THE 12 NOTES OF MUSIC
Music Theory Simplified: Ear Training And Interval Study Course
CONCEIVED AND WRITTEN BY MARK JOHN STERNAL

MJS Music & Entertainment, LLC

www.MJSPublications.com

ISBN 978-0-9817451-0-7

(Previous Edition 978-0-9762917-2-5)

For distribution contact:
MJS Music & Entertainment, LLC
9699 W Fort Island Trail
Crystal River, FL 34429
(352)-563-1779

Written and arranged by Mark John Sternal.
Edited by Mark and Jeanne Sternal

COPYRIGHT CONDITIONS

NO PART OF THIS BOOK MAY BE REPRODUCED WITHOUT WRITTEN CONSENT FROM THE PUBLISHER.

COPYRIGHT FOR ORIGINAL MANUSCRIPT AUGUST, 1998 MJS
MANUSCRIPT REVISED JUNE 2001
FILED WITH THE LIBRARY OF CONGRESS, COPYRIGHT 2004
UNITED STATES PATENT APPLIED FOR 2004
LATEST REVISION, MARCH, 2010

© 2010 DELUXE REVISION

Dear Musician,

Thank you and congratulations for choosing "The Twelve Notes Of Music." Although this is a short book, the information written on it's pages is priceless. I devised this concept of ear training while I was teaching music full time in Florida. Interval study is nothing new, but a patterned system for learning each interval in every key, on every guitar or bass string and fret, or every key on a piano, makes it easier than ever. I have been using "The Twelve Notes Of Music" system with my students since 1997 and their progress has been amazing! Their ability to learn by ear has increased dramatically and much faster than I expected. It has also resulted in more creative, melodic and harmonic song writing and improvisation. My students and I are finding we can name intervals, (melody, harmony and chords), just by hearing them.

For example: You are listening to a song and you notice that the progression uses Perfect Fourth passing chords for the first two measures, then a Minor Sixth interval played as a major chord, followed by a Major Third, then a Perfect Fifth played as a diminished chord, (which theoretically does not fit, but it sounds perfect in this particular song). If I'm losing you here, please do not get discouraged! After you have studied the interval patterns in this book, you will have a complete understanding of these references and a much deeper appreciation for music.

The same applies for writing music. When writing a melody, harmony or chords, you will begin to find it easier to choose the next note or group of notes to add to your song. Overall, expressing your musical thoughts will become second nature. With practice, you will be able to do it instantly.

Here's how it works: After establishing a root note, there are only 12 intervals that can apply. Spend enough time on each interval and learn to recognize it's qualities. When you begin to study the next interval, compare it with the intervals you have already studied and learn their differences. After you have learned all twelve intervals, choose another note as a root and apply the patterns to this new musical key. After you have learned a few musical keys, you will find the remainder of the 12 keys will get progressively easier and may not even require much effort at all. That is the beauty of these patterns. They never change! Regardless of what key you are in, a perfect fifth interval will always be a perfect fifth interval.

If you don't understand what is written on this page, read it again after you have applied the 12 easy steps in this book. It will make a world of sense to you at that time.

I wish you the best success with your musical pursuit, whether it's your career or hobby!

Sincerely,

Mark John Sternal

THE 12 NOTES OF MUSIC
Music Theory Simplified: Ear Training And Interval Study Course
TABLE OF CONTENTS

INTRO.....4
MUSIC.....4
CHAPTER 1: PICK A NOTE, ANY NOTE!.....4
THE FIRST, 1, I, THE ROOT, THE TONIC.....4
CHAPTER 2.....5
THE FLAT SECOND, THE MINOR SECOND, Semi Tone, b2, bii, ii.....5
Playing a b2 Harmony on Guitar or Bass.....5
CHAPTER 3.....6
THE SECOND, 2, II.....6
Playing a 2 Harmony on Guitar or Bass.....6
CHAPTER 4.....6
THE MINOR THIRD, m3, IIIm, b3, iii.....6
CHAPTER 5.....7
THE MAJOR THIRD, 3, III.....7
CHAPTER 6.....7
THE PERFECT FORTH, FOURTH, 4, P4, IV.....7
INTERVAL SYMBOLS.....8
THE PERFECT FORTH, FOURTH, 4, P4, IV.....8
CHAPTER 7.....8
THE AUGMENTED FOURTH, SHARP FOURTH, AUG 4, #4, IV+.....8
THE DIMINISHED FIFTH, FLAT FIVE, dim5, b5, V°.....8
CHAPTER 8.....9
THE PERFECT FIFTH, FIFTH, 5, P5, V.....9
CHAPTER 9.....9
THE AUGMENTED FIFTH, SHARP FIVE, AUG 5, #5, V+.....9
ENHARMONIC.....9
THE MINOR SIXTH, FLAT SIX, b6, m6, VIm, bVI, vi.....9
CHAPTER 10.....10
THE MAJOR SIXTH, 6, VI.....10
DIMINISHED SEVENTH, dim 7, bb7(Double Flat Seven), vii°.....10
CHAPTER 11.....10
MINOR SEVENTH, FLAT SEVEN, m7, b7, VIIm, vii.....10
CHAPTER 12.....11
THE MAJOR SEVENTH, 7, VII.....11
CHAPTER 1 / 13.....11
THE OCTAVE, 8va, 8 / 1, THE FIRST, 1, I, THE ROOT NOTE, THE TONIC.....11
MORE ABOUT ROOT NOTES...12
RESOLUTION.....12
ESTABLISH A STRONG MUSICAL EAR.....12
LEARNING A SONG BY EAR.....13
IF IT IS A CHORD OR HARMONY YOU ARE BUILDING.....13
INTERVAL PATTERNS USED FOR COMMON SCALES AND CHORDS.....13
THE MUSICAL ALPHABET.....16
THE MUSICAL ALPHABET AND THE GUITAR, BASS, AND PIANO.....16
MUSICAL KEY AND INTERVAL CHART.....16
GUITAR INTERVAL CHART AND FRETBOARD NOTE CHART.....17
BASS INTERVAL CHART AND FRETBOARD NOTE CHART.....18
A NOTE FROM THE AUTHOR...18
BONUS BEGINNER LESSON: READING NOTE CHARTS.....19
GUITAR AND BASS GUITAR COMPARISON.....19

THE TWELVE NOTES OF MUSIC

INTRO

Although there are many frets on a guitar, (6 string, 12 string or bass), or many keys on a piano... the fact is there are only 12 notes in the musical alphabet. This narrows music down to only 12 basic possibilities. Once you have learned each possibility, you will have complete control over your instrument and any musical circumstance.

MARK JOHN STERNAL

MUSIC

Music is the study of time and sound. Here we are studying sound. To be more precise, we are studying the relationship between notes. There are 4 terms we need to learn.

The first term is **Interval**. An **Interval** is how music is measured, or the distance between notes. Just like the difference between colors –the contrast of light and dark, or bright and dull to our eyes –there is a recognizable difference, (or distance), between musical notes to our ears. The key word in the last sentence is "recognizable." You can learn to recognize musical notes / tones and their association to each other!

Our second term is **Melody**, which is a group of single notes played in any order.

Our next term is **Harmony**, which is when you have more than one note being played at the same time.

Chord is our fourth musical term used in the "Twelve Notes Of Music" system. A **Chord** is three or more different tones played together at the same time.

CHAPTER 1: PICK A NOTE, ANY NOTE!

THE FIRST – 1 – I – THE ROOT – THE TONIC

The First, or Root Note, is unquestionably, unarguably, the most important note of music. It is the note on which we base all other notes. The Root is the base upon which all scales, melodies, harmonies and chords are built. It is the note which names what key we are in. It is the most resolving note in a group of notes. The lack of it makes the listener want to hear it even more. **To find it on your instrument, simply play a note.** *If your instrument is a guitar or bass, choose a string, choose a fret and play it. If you are a pianist, choose a key, white or black. That one note by itself with no other notes played before, with, or after it, to influence its sound, is your Root

Note. The note you are playing may be a Gb, or an E, or a C note. It does not matter. Remember where it is and use it as your foundation throughout this book.
*If it is your first time applying this method, choose a Root Note on strings 3 through 6 of your guitar, or strings 3 or 4 on a bass guitar.

CHAPTER 2

THE FLAT SECOND – MINOR SECOND – Semi Tone – b2 – bII – ii

The Flat Second interval is a half step higher in pitch from the Root. A half step is one fret up or down on a guitar or bass and one key up or down on a piano.

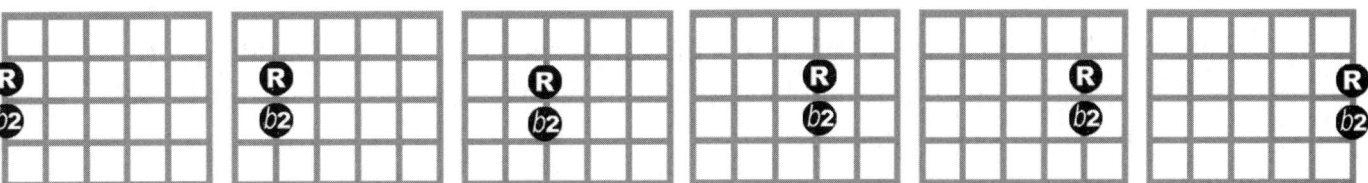

On any string of a guitar, a b2 interval looks like this. Find the chart that applies to your root note.
TIP FOR BEGINNERS: If you do not yet know how to read note charts, please see our easy tutorial on page 19.
BASS PLAYERS: The guitar charts used in this book can be applied to bass guitar by ignoring any notes played on the high B and E strings (2 & 1). If you are not sure how to do this, see page 19.

A b2 interval is the shortest of intervals. The sound quality of just these two notes played in sequence has a minor feel or sound. The two notes played together as a harmony has a strong dissonance. Dissonance can be defined as undesirable or unresolved.
TIP: To resolve the strong dissonance of a b2 harmony, or any dissonant tone, follow it with a single root note.

Playing a b2 Harmony on Guitar or Bass

Since harmony notes must be played together, they have to be played on separate strings for guitar or bass. This will also give you another option for playing a b2 melody.

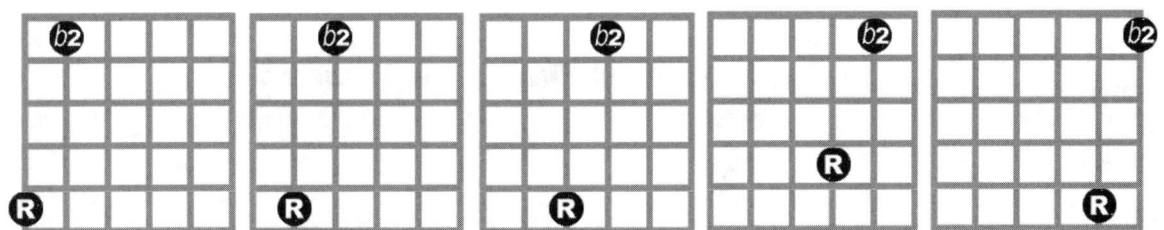

A b2 harmony looks like this on a guitar. Find the chart that applies to your root note. Apply the proper fingering to match these fret and string distances, then play both notes together.

CHAPTER 3

THE SECOND, 2, II

A Second interval is a whole step higher in pitch than the root note. A whole step is equal to two frets up or down on a guitar or bass, or two keys on a piano. Played as a melody, a Second is the most commonly found interval in music.

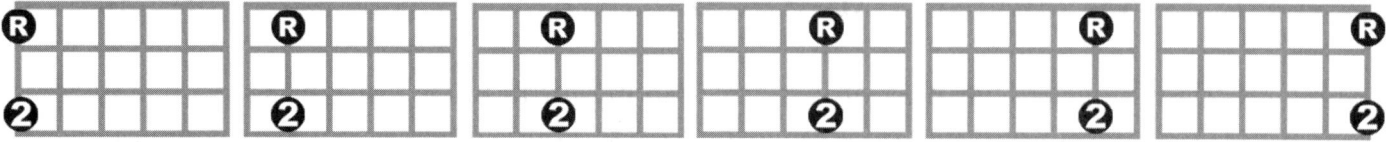

On any string of a guitar, a 2 interval looks like this.

The sound quality of these two notes played in sequence has a neutral quality. It can lead to a major or minor quality depending on what other notes, if any, are added to it's interval. The sound quality of a Second harmony is defined as soft dissonance.

Playing a 2 Harmony on Guitar or Bass

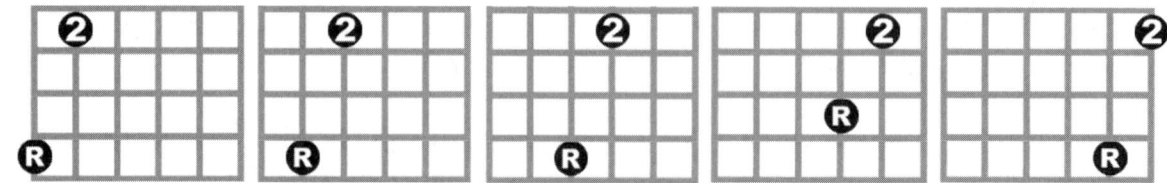

A 2 harmony looks like this on a guitar. Find the chart that applies to your root note. Apply the proper fingering to match these fret and string distances, then play both notes together.

CHAPTER 4

THE MINOR THIRD, m3, IIIm, b3, iii

A Minor Third interval is one-and-a-half steps in distance. A One-and-a-half step interval is 3 frets on a guitar or bass, or 3 keys on a piano. The Minor Third melody is used commonly in all musical styles, including classical, blues, rock and country. Both the Minor Third melody and harmony give a sad or mellow emotion to music. As a harmony, the Minor Third is one of the most commonly used intervals.

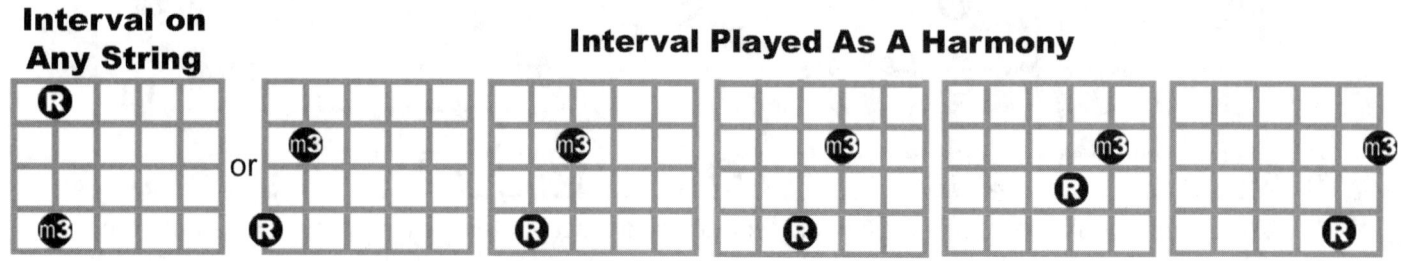

A minor third looks like this on the guitar.

CHAPTER 5

THE MAJOR THIRD, 3, III

A Major Third interval is two steps in distance, 4 frets on a guitar or bass, 4 keys on a piano. Like the minor third, the Major Third is used widely in blues, rock, pop, and also country music. Also, like the minor third, the Major Third has an emotional sound quality. The emotion portrayed by a Major Third harmony or melody is bright or happy. As a harmony it is one of the most popular intervals.

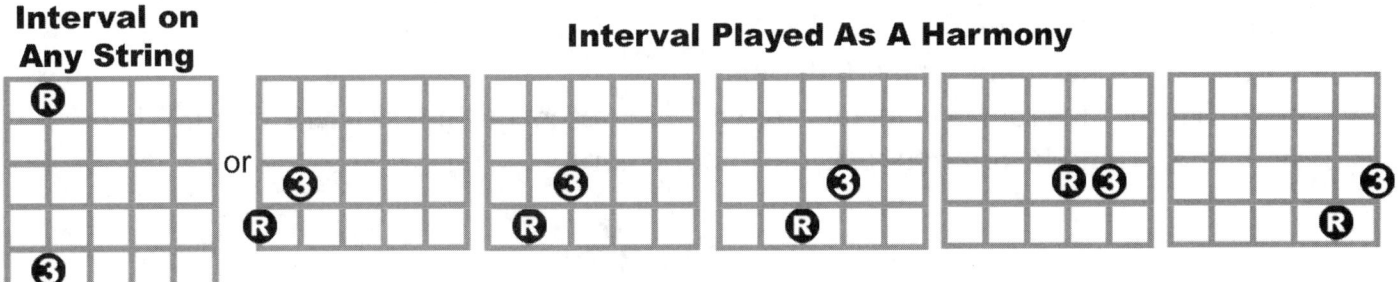

Major Third intervals look like this on a guitar.

CHAPTER 6

THE PERFECT FOURTH, FOURTH, 4, P4, IV

The Perfect Fourth is two-and-a-half steps, 5 frets, or 5 keys distance. The 4th is a neutral tone. It does note have a major or minor quality, (or emotion), to it's sound. Because of this, a 4th harmony or melody can be used in almost any musical situation.

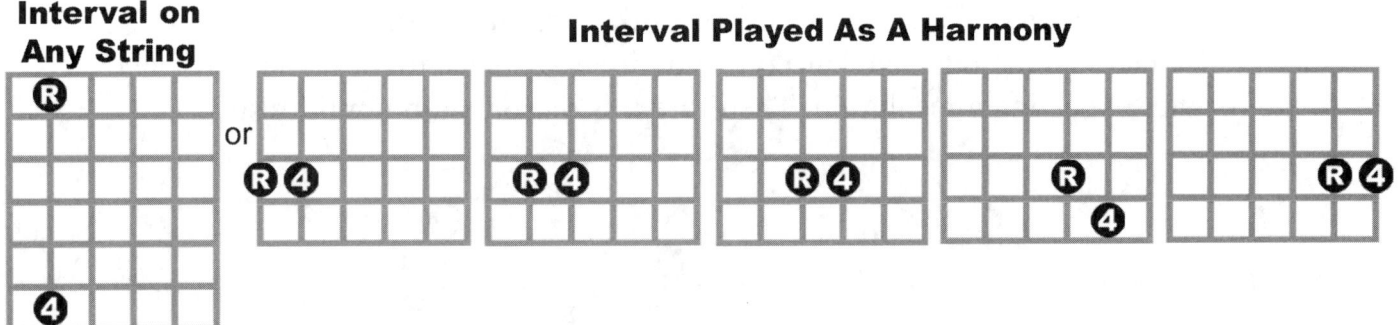

Here is what a perfect 4 interval looks like on a guitar. You may find the stretch difficult to play a Root to 4 interval on the same string. For this reason, the remaining intervals will be written on separate strings.

When played as a chord, the IV chord is the second most popular chord used in music. The most popular chord in music would obviously be the I chord.

-----INTERVAL SYMBOLS-----

Now that you have some experience with intervals and their numeric quality, let us take a look at the application of their symbols. Our example will be the title of this chapter.

THE PERFECT FOURTH, FOURTH, 4, P4, IV

In written music or spoken musical terms, perfect fourth, fourth, P4 and 4 would represent the individual note in a given key. If specified, it would also represent the harmony of a given key.
Example: P4 harmony, or fourth harmony.
The written roman numeral, IV, would represent that interval as a chord. When spoken, it would be referred to as the "Four Chord."

CHAPTER 7

THE AUGMENTED FOURTH, SHARP FOURTH, AUG 4, #4, IV+ ENHARMONIC

An Augmented Fourth is an Enharmonic interval. Enharmonic means a note with more than one name. The other name for an Augmented Fourth interval is a Diminished Fifth.

THE DIMINISHED FIFTH, FLAT FIVE, dim5, b5, V°

The Augmented Fourth/Diminished Fifth interval is three steps, six frets, six keys distance. It's melodic and harmonic quality is suspenseful or restless. It leaves the listener expecting a resolution. Therefore it is dissonant, but mildly so.

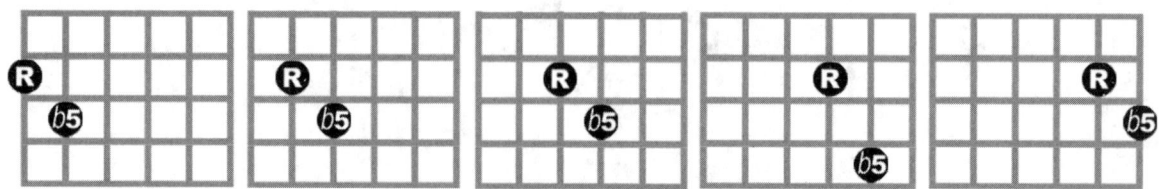

An Augmented Fourth/Diminished Fifth interval looks like this on the guitar.

TIP: Why Enharmonic? The reason for Enharmonic notes is to avoid repeating an interval number. **For Example:** You would not want to have a scale that consists of the intervals 1-2-3-4-#4. Since the 4 is already established, you would call the next note a b5. The proper writing would be: 1-2-3-4-b5.
On the other hand, if the 4 has not been established, but the #4/b5 is present, you would name the interval based on the lowest available number, as in 1-2-3-#4.
When using the *musical alphabet, it is also important not to repeat alphabetical notes in a scale. For example, avoid A-B-C-C#, by calling C# by it's enharmonic name, Db. The correct writing would be A-B-C-Db.
*See page 16, The Musical Alphabet.

CHAPTER 8

THE PERFECT FIFTH, FIFTH, 5, P5, V

A Perfect Fifth is three-and-a-half steps, 7 frets, 7 keys distance. The tonal quality of a Fifth melody or harmony is neutral. It does not have a major or minor emotion, so it can be used in either situation. A Fifth has an aggressive character to it's sound, which is resolving to the listener. It is the opposite of dissonant, which is consonant. Previous examples of consonant intervals are the 1, b3, 3, and the 4.

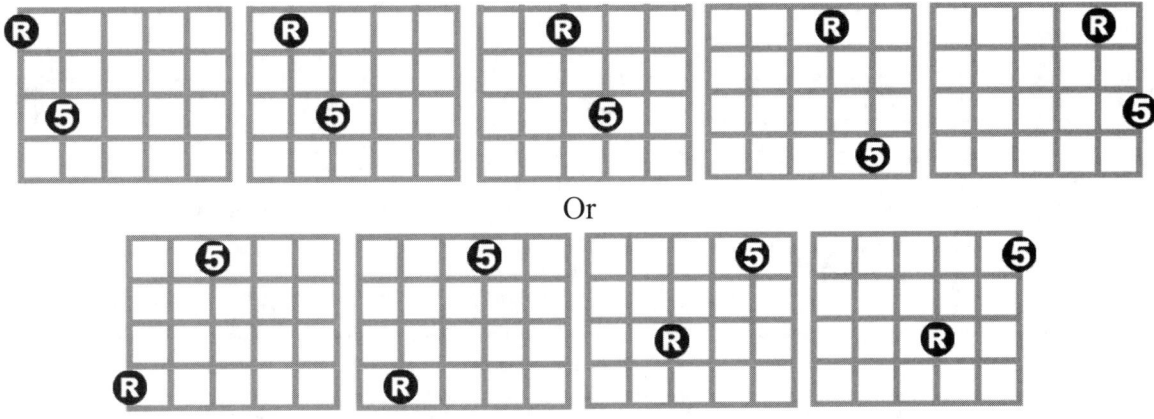

CHAPTER 9

THE AUGMENTED FIFTH, SHARP FIVE, AUG 5, #5, V+
ENHARMONIC
THE MINOR SIXTH, FLAT SIX, b6, m6, VIm, bVI, vi

An Augmented Fifth is enharmonic to the Minor Sixth. The distance of this interval is four steps, 8 frets, or 8 keys. It's melodic and harmonic quality is suspenseful and unresolved. A #5/b6 is for the most part dissonant, but there are times when it's use with other intervals will give it a mild consonance.

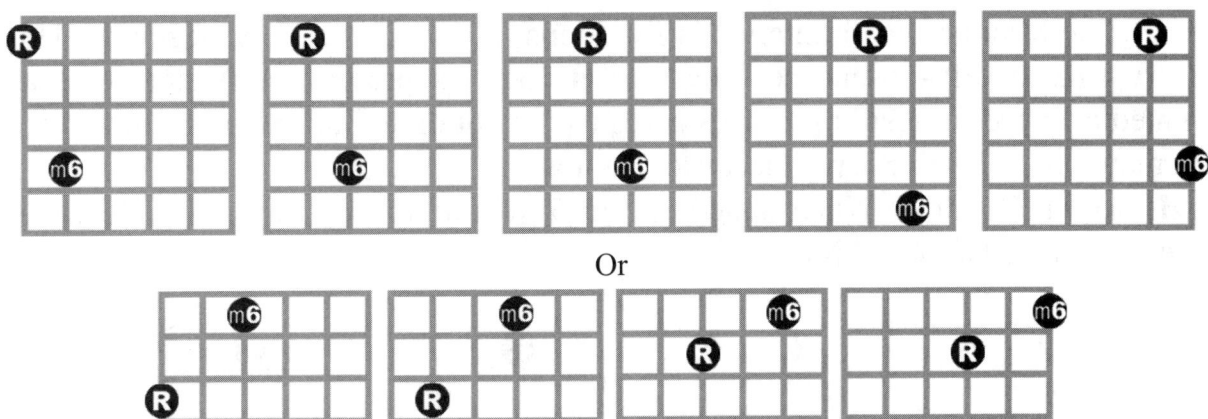

CHAPTER 10

THE MAJOR SIXTH, 6, VI
ENHARMONIC
DIMINISHED SEVENTH, dim 7, bb7(Double Flat Seven), vii°

The Major Sixth/Diminished Seventh interval is four-and-a-half steps, 9 frets, or 9 keys distance. The sound quality is subtle, giving it a mild consonance. This melody or harmony will allow the listener to accept any other major interval.

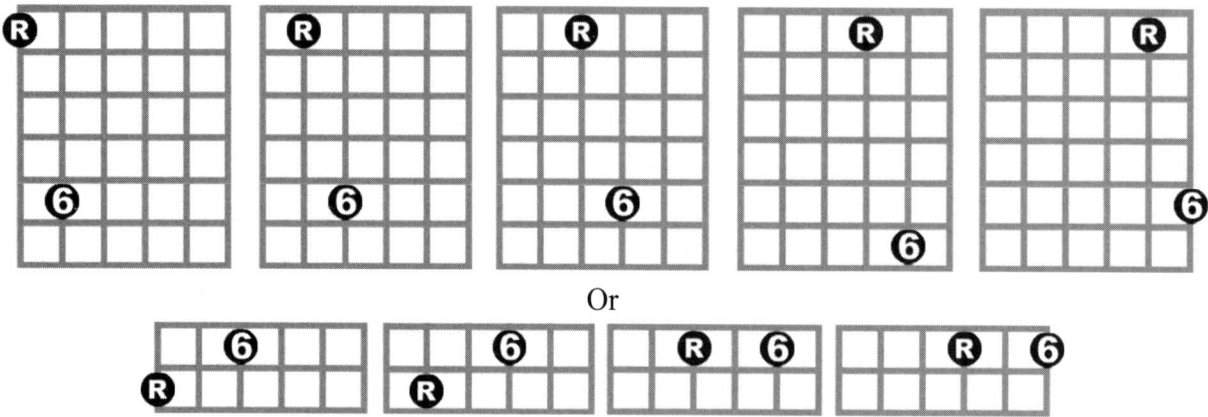

Or

CHAPTER 11

MINOR SEVENTH, FLAT SEVEN, SEVEN, 7, m7, b7, VIIm, vii

The Minor Seventh interval is five steps, 10 frets, or 10 keys distance. This interval has a soft dissonance. However, it does not present the listener with an immediate need for resolution. This gives us the option to build upon its melody or harmony, or to resolve it with a consonant note.

CHORD THEORY: When added to the 5th chord in any key, this interval is considered the DOMINANT 7.

CHAPTER 12

THE MAJOR SEVENTH, ^7, M7

The Major Seventh is five-and-a-half steps, 11 frets, or 11 keys distance. A Major Seventh is often referred to as the leading tone. It is the furthest interval from the root note and is the closest to the next octave. It's strong dissonant melody and harmony lead the listener to expect a resolution. Any dissonant interval can be resolved by any consonant tone. The strongest consonance being that of the root.

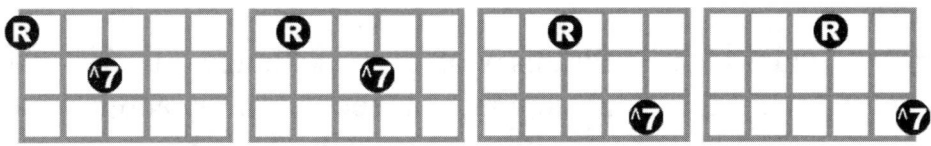

CHAPTER 1 / 13

THE OCTAVE, 8va, 8/1, THE FIRST, 1, I, THE ROOT NOTE, THE TONIC

Welcome back to chapter one. The Octave is the same note and has the same name as the Root Note. The difference between the two notes is the frequency. An Octave note is double or half the frequency of a given note. The Octave is six steps, 12 frets, or 12 keys in distance. Here, at the octave, is where we apply our interval knowledge over again. This allows us to expand our musical possibilities and capabilities even further. This is how we are able to play a combination of the same 12 notes in different positions on an 88 key piano, or on a 24 fret, 6 string guitar or 4 string bass guitar.

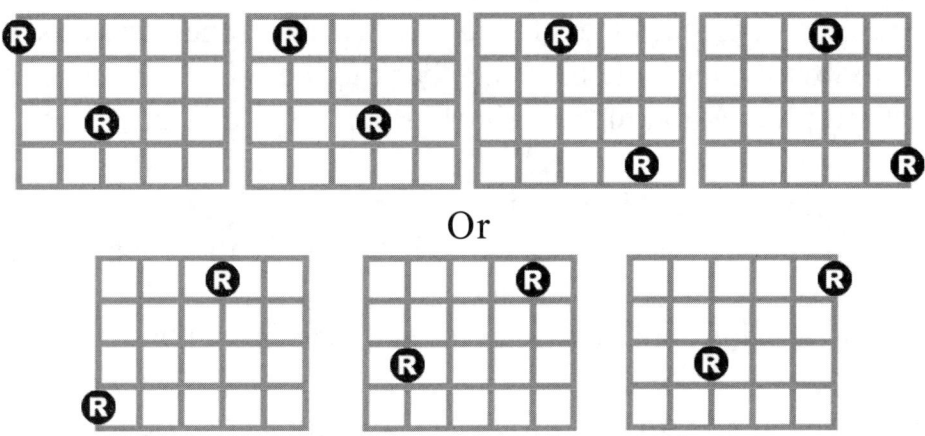

Or

MORE ABOUT ROOT NOTES:

As stated in Chapter 1, the Root Note is the most important note when building intervals. It is our foundation. In creating music, it is equally important to remember the Root Note or 1st does not necessarily have to be played before any other note. Many songs begin on the 4th or 5th. Many creative artists avoid playing the Root to make the listener anticipate it in a song. Sometimes the lack of the Root will make it sound even more bold when a song finally does resolve to it's use.

RESOLUTION

There was and is no need for this book to be any longer than it is. Again, there are only 12 notes and there is only so much someone can say about these 12 notes. These 12 intervals we have covered are nothing new. They have existed as long as music itself. If this is your first time through this book your job in not finished yet.
1. Apply what you now know to every possible octave of your root note.
2. Use these 12 intervals to master every key in music.

TO ESTABLISH A STRONG MUSICAL EAR...

1. listen for the recognizable traits to each interval in all 12 keys.
2. Compare a fourth to a fifth, or a minor third to a major third. Do this to all the intervals in every key.
3. Recognize the uniqueness that every interval has.
4. Use famous songs to remember each interval quality. Even in different keys the interval quality does not change.

For example: The main theme from the "Star Wars" soundtrack starts with a 1st to a 5th, then to a 4th, 3rd, 2nd, 8va, then back to the 5th.

The guitar riff from the blues classic "Bad To The Bone" uses a 1st to a perfect 4th interval, followed by a 1st to b3rd then back to the 1st.

The chord progression to "Jail House Rock" is I to ii, both played as major chords.

The intro guitar riff to "If 6 Was 9" by Jimi Hendrix is a I to II melody.

The unforgettable music from the movie "Jaws" is a 1 to 8va to a b2nd played as an octave.

With practice you will find interval associations with songs that you are familiar with.

You can use the knowledge found in this book to produce every melody, harmony, and chord imaginable!

WHEN YOU ARE LEARNING A SONG BY EAR...

1. All you need is one note from the song.
2. If it is a lead or melody you are learning just apply different intervals until you have found the correct note.

IF IT IS A CHORD OR HARMONY YOU ARE BUILDING

1. First find the note that stands out the most.
2. Then listen for a harmony that fits.
3. When you find the first harmony, listen for the other note or notes that are present in the chord.

TIP: Most harmonies and chords will include the 1, 3 and 5 or the 1, b3 and 5.

As with anything, you will get better and quicker with time and even find yourself going directly to the note you are looking for.

INTERVAL PATTERNS USED FOR COMMON SCALES AND CHORDS

SCALES:

MAJOR = 1, 2, 3, 4, 5, 6, ^7, 8/1   MINOR = 1, 2, b3, 4, 5, b6, 7, 8/1

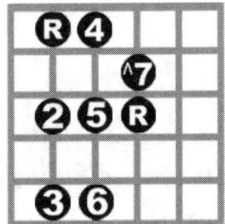   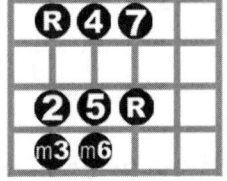

MAJOR PENTATONIC   MINOR PENTATONIC
= 1, 2, 3, 5, 6, 8/1   = 1, b3, 4, 5, 7, 8/1

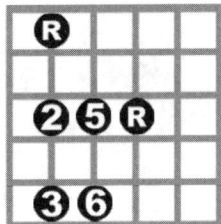   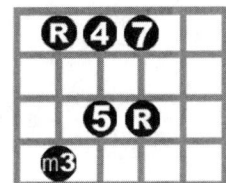

CHORDS:

MAJOR = 1, 3, 5

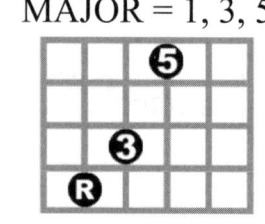

MINOR = 1, b3, 5

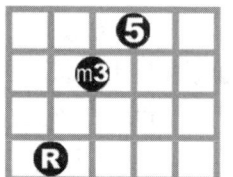

DIMINISHED = 1, b3, b5

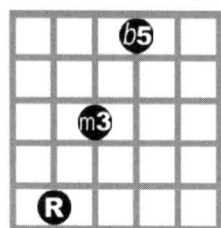

AUGMENTED = 1, 3, #5

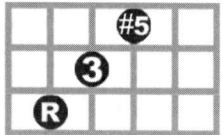

EXTENDED CHORD FORMULAS
Seventh Chords

We know a chord is made up of 3 or more notes. The formula for a triad is to use the 1-3 and 5th interval. The next chord extension above a triad is to build a 7th chord, consisting of the 1-3-5 and 7th interval.

MAJOR SEVENTH = 1, 3, 5, ^7
MINOR SEVENTH = 1, b3, 5, 7
DOMINANT SEVENTH CHORDS = 1, 3, 5, 7

COMPOUND INTERVALS
1 - 2 - 3 - 4 - 5 - 6 - 7 - 8/1 - 9/2 - 10/3 - 11/4 - 12/5 - 13/6

An interval greater than an octave is called a Compound Interval. These intervals become necessary when building chords beyond seventh chords.

NINTH CHORDS

The reason for using a 9th interval is to build a 5 note chord beyond 7th chords. When we combine the 1-3-5-7-9 intervals, we now have 9th chords. The 9 interval is the same as the 2 interval.

MAJOR NINTH = 1, 3, 5, ^7, 9/2
MINOR NINTH = 1, b3, 5, 7, 9
NINTH = 1, 3, 5, 7, 9

TENTH AND TWELVE CHORDS

There are no tenth or twelve chords in music theory. Since the basic foundation of a chord consists of the 1-3-5 intervals, when you compound intervals, these notes are already present. The 3rd would be the 10th compound interval and 5th would be the 12th compound interval.

ELEVENTH CHORDS

To build the Eleventh Chord, we would create a maj11 by combining 1-3-5-^7-9-11. This chord is often altered by raising the 11th interval to a #11 resulting in a maj9(#11) chord.
A m11 chord would use the intervals 1-b3-5-7-9-11.
An 11 chord would use 1-3-5-7-9-11.

THIRTEENTH CHORDS

For guitar music, Thirteenth chords usually do not include the 11th interval. When it does, the chord name must list the type of 11th interval used. For example, if a C13 chord included a #11th interval, you would call the chord a C Major 13 (#11).
If the 11th interval is not specified, as in C Major 13, you will omit the 11th interval. The formula for a Major 13 chord is 1-3-5-^7-9-13.
A minor 13 chord is 1-b3-5-7-9-13.
The formula for a 13 chord is 1-3-5-7-9-13.

SUSPENDED CHORDS

When a chord is lacking a 3rd interval, it is considered a suspended chord. The lack of a 3rd interval creates a neutral feel to the chord because it is not major or minor.

SUSPENDED TWO = 1, 2, 5
SUSPENDED FOUR = 1, 4, 5

2 OR ADD 2 CHORDS

By taking an existing triad and adding a 2nd interval you are creating a 2 or Add 2 chord.

MAJOR SECOND = 1, 2, 3, 5
MINOR SECOND = 1, 2, b3, 5

6 CHORDS

A triad plus a 6th interval will make a 6 chord.

MAJOR SIXTH = 1, 3, 5, 6
MINOR SIXTH = 1, b3, 5, 6

6/9 CHORDS

By playing a 6 chord and adding the 2nd or 9th interval, the chord becomes a 6/9 chord. To be a 6/9 chord, the 7th interval cannot be present.

MAJOR 6/9 = 1-3-5-6-9
MINOR 6/9 = 1-b3-5-6-9

THE MUSICAL ALPHABET

The musical alphabet consists of 12 notes.

A	A#/Bb	B	C	C#/Db	D	D#/Eb	E	F	F#/Gb	G	G#/Ab	A
1	2	3	4	5	6	7	8	9	10	11	12	1

The notes **A, B, C, D, E, F, & G** are called basic or <u>natural</u> notes.

The notes **A#/Bb, C#/Db, D#/Eb, F#/Gb and G#/Ab** are called <u>accidentals</u>.

THE MUSICAL ALPHABET AND THE GUITAR, BASS OR PIANO

GUITAR: Each of the six strings of the guitar have been assigned a specific note. The 6th string, which is the top and heaviest string is an E note. It is called the low E string. When this string is properly tuned and played OPEN, (no frets), it will produce an E pitch. Each fret after that will bring you to the next note in the musical alphabet.

EXAMPLE. If you play the 1st fret of the 6th string it will produce the F note, the 2nd fret will produce a F#/Gb note, 3rd fret will produce a G note, next a G#/Ab note, then A, the 6th fret will be an A#/Bb note, 7th fret B, 8th C, Etc. Once you reach the 12th fret, the musical alphabet will repeat itself starting with the E note. The 5th string open is an A note. The 4th string is a D note, 3rd string is a G note, 2nd is the B string and the 1st string is the high E string.

BASS: Standard tuning on a bass guitar is one octave lower than guitar with E for the 4th or heaviest string. The third string open is an A note, 2nd string open is a D note and the first string open is a G note.

PIANO: On a Piano, the white keys are natural notes and the black keys are the sharps and flats. The black keys are in groups of two and three. The white key between the group of 2 black keys is always a D note. When you ascend in pitch from left to right, each key will produce the next note in the musical alphabet.

MUSICAL KEY AND INTERVAL CHART

This chart shows each interval in every key.

KEY	1	b2	2	b3	3	4	#4/b5	5	#5/m6	6/ bb7	b7	^7	8/1
A	A	Bb	B	C	C#	D	D#/Eb	E	E#/F	F#/Gb	G	G#	A
Bb	Bb	B	C	Db	D	Eb	E/Fb	F	F#/Gb	G/Abb	Ab	A	Bb
B	B	C	C#	D	D#	E	E#/F	F#	F##/G	G#/Ab	A	A#	B
C	C	Db	D	D#	E	F	F#/Gb	G	G#/Ab	A/Bbb	Bb	B	C
C#	C#	D	D#	E	E#	F#	F##/G	G#	G##/A	A#/Bb	B	B#	C#
D	D	Eb	E	F	F#	G	G#/Ab	A	A#/Bb	B/Cb	C	C#	D
Eb	Eb	Fb	F	Gb	G	Ab	A/Bbb	Bb	B/Cb	C/Dbb	Db	D	Eb
E	E	F	F#	G	G#	A	A#/Bb	B	B#/C	C#/Db	D	D#	E
F	F	Gb	G	Ab	A	Bb	B/Cb	C	C#/Db	D/Ebb	Eb	E	F
F#	F#	G	G#	A	A#	B	B#/C	C#	C##/D	D#/Eb	E	E#	F#
G	G	Ab	A	Bb	B	C	C#/Db	D	D#/Eb	E/Fb	F	F#	G
Ab	Ab	Bbb	Bb	Cb	C	Db	D/Ebb	Eb	E/Fb	F/Gbb	Gb	G	Ab

GUITAR INTERVAL CHART AND FRETBOARD NOTE CHART

INTERVALS

m3	m6	b2	b5	7	m3
3	6	2	5	^7	3
4	7	m3	m6	R	4
b5	^7	3	6	b2	b5
5	R	4	7	2	5
m6	b2	b5	^7	m3	m6
6	2	5	R	3	6
7	m3	m6	b2	4	7
^7	3	6	2	b5	^7
R	4	7	m3	5	R
b2	b5	^7	3	m6	b2
2	5	R	4	6	2

This image contains a Guitar Fretboard Interval Chart. Notice that individual **fret numbers have not been given**. This will allow you to quickly find intervals and their octaves in any key.

FRETBOARD NOTE CHART

Open	E	A	D	G	B	E	12th Fret
1st Fret	F	A#/Bb	D#/Eb	G#/Ab	C	F	13th Fret
2nd Fret	F#/Gb	B	E	A	C#/Db	F#/Gb	14th Fret
3rd Fret	G	C	F	A#/Bb	D	G	15th Fret
4th Fret	G#/Ab	C#/Db	F#/Gb	B	D#/Eb	G#/Ab	16th Fret
5th Fret	A	D	G	C	E	A	17th Fret
6th Fret	A#/Bb	D#/Eb	G#/Ab	C#/Db	F	A#/Bb	18th Fret
7th Fret	B	E	A	D	F#/Gb	B	19th Fret
8th Fret	C	F	A#/Bb	D#/Eb	G	C	20th Fret
9th Fret	C#/Db	F#/Gb	B	E	G#/Ab	C#/Db	21st Fret
10th Fret	D	G	C	F	A	D	22nd Fret
11th Fret	D#/Eb	G#/Ab	C#/Db	F#/Gb	A#/Bb	D#/Eb	23rd Fret
12th Fret	E	A	D	G	B	E	24th Fret

This image contains a Fretboard Note Chart for guitar. The left side of the chart shows the fret numbers for the first octave, frets Open through 12. The right side shows the fret numbers for the second octave, frets 12 through 24.

BASS GUITAR INTERVAL CHART AND FRETBOARD NOTE CHART

INTERVALS

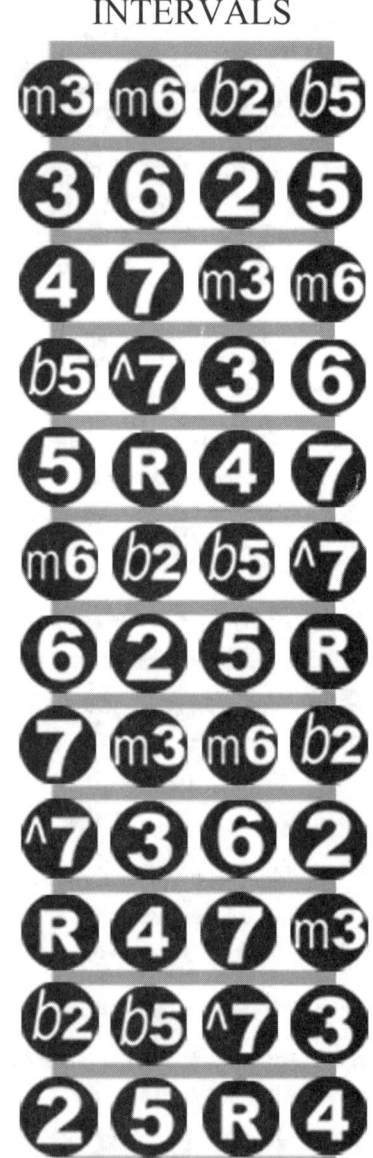

FRETBOARD NOTE CHART

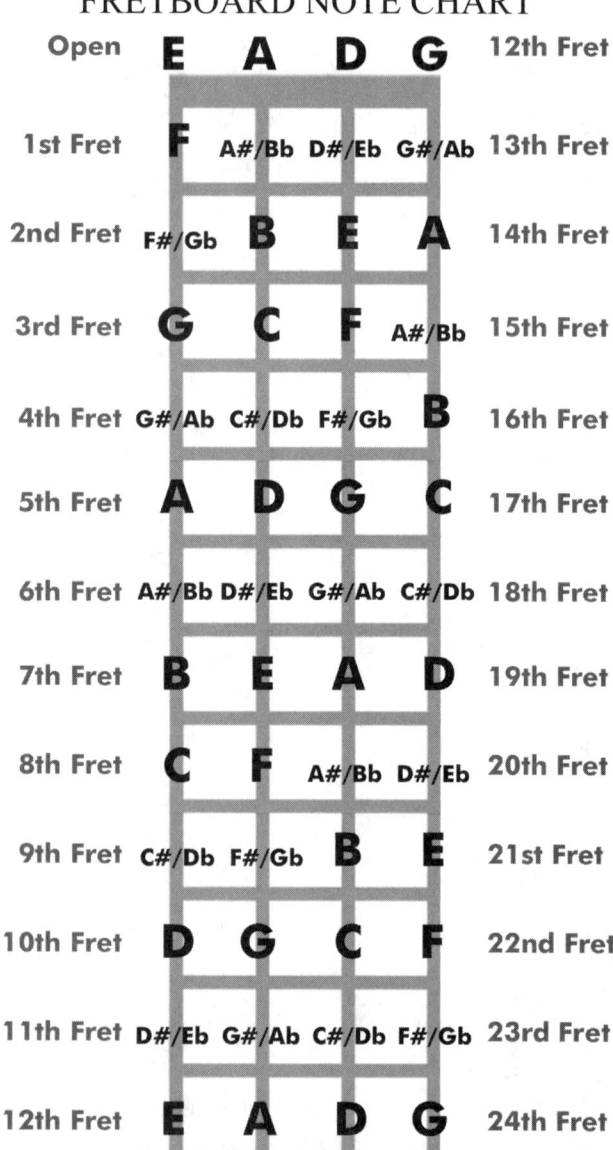

This image contains a Bass Guitar Fretboard Interval Chart. Notice that individual **fret numbers have not been given**. This will allow you to quickly find intervals and their octaves in any key.

This image contains a Fretboard Note Chart for guitar. The left side of the chart shows the fret numbers for the first octave, frets Open through 12. The right side shows the fret numbers for the second octave, frets 12 through 24.

A NOTE FROM THE AUTHOR

Fellow Musician,

    I hope you have enjoyed "The Twelve Notes Of Music" system. With each passing day, I pray your knowledge and awareness of interval relationships will grow stronger. Listen for them in your practice and your enjoyment of all music. It is my wish for you that your musical ability will become all that you dream it to be.

MARK JOHN STERNAL

BONUS BEGINNER LESSON:
READING NOTE CHARTS

strings

Each vertical line represents a guitar string. The thinnest string is #1, through the thickest string being #6.

frets

Each horizontal line represents a fret

FRET MARKERS

Dots are placed on the note chart as fret markers to show you which strings and frets to hold in order to play scales or chords. In some cases, like the example to the left, hollow dots on a note chart represent an open string.

The note chart to the left shows three dots on the first string. The dots represent the notes to play on the fretboard. To play these notes, simply pick the first string open, then the first fret, then the third fret. You can also play the notes descending by picking the first string third fret, then first fret, then open.

GUITAR AND BASS GUITAR COMPARISON

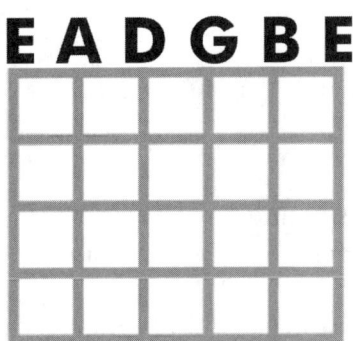

Traditional 6-string guitars are tuned from the 6th string open as E A D G B E.

Traditional 4-string bass guitars are tuned from the 4th string open as E A D G.

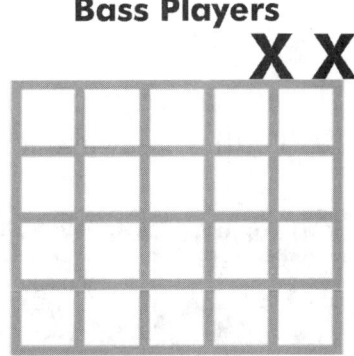

Since the low strings, E A D G match on both guitar and bass guitar, bass players can use guitar charts by ignoring any charts that involve the high B and E strings.

ABOUT THE AUTHOR

Photo courtesy of MJS Music & Entertainment, LLC. Taken by Scott Hunt. Mark on the set of GUITAR DVD #1: Beginner Basics and Beyond, 2010.

Expert Guitar Instructor Mark John Sternal is the author of over 25 best selling guitar and bass instructional titles. Mark began teaching his trademark method to private students in 1991. He was only 17, with one year left of high school before he would attend Richard Daley College in Chicago. By 1994, Mark had relocated to Florida and with him came the manuscript for his first book. Fueled by glowing user feedback and testimonials from thousands of satisfied customers, Mark's growing number of music instruction titles awarded him national recognition in 2004. Since then, his titles have consistently held the #1 best selling music instruction slots at some of the largest music and book stores in the United States.

OTHER TITLES

If you enjoyed The Twelve Notes Of Music, you are going to love the other book and DVD titles by Mark John Sternal.

891926002014   891926002069

GUITAR DVD #1: Beginner Basics and Beyond
BASS GUITAR DVD #1: Beginner Basics and Beyond

Includes all you need to survive in the world of guitar or bass! Designed to be the FASTEST and EASIEST way to learn to play, GUARANTEED! Learn to read sheet music with notation, TAB and charts. Start playing instantly, learning individual notes, while gradually speeding up to full chords (guitar). Then graduate to your first 5 SONGS in the most popular music styles including Rock, Blues and Country.

TOTAL SCALES TECHNIQUES AND APPLICATIONS

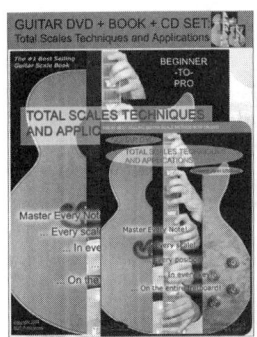
DVD/BOOK/CD set
978-0976291787

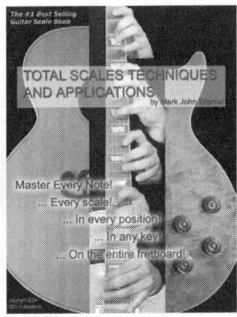
Guitar Book/CD
978-0976291701

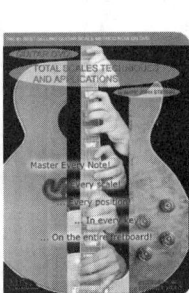
Guitar DVD
891926002007

Bass Book/CD
978-0976291756

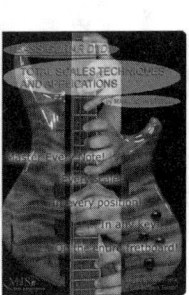
Bass DVD
891926002052

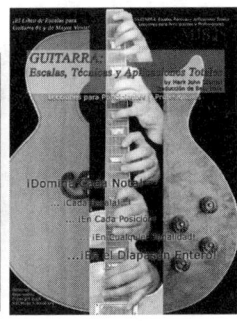
Spanish Book
978-0976291718

Know by musicians throughout the world as TSTA, Total Scales Techniques and Applications is recommended for every guitarist and bassist, regardless of playing level or musical taste! It starts with all the basics a beginner needs to know and moves progressively through advanced and professional level techniques and applications. It is a scale encyclopedia, but more importantly it shows every possible way of using the scales to make music. You learn to play in every key and use every position on the fretboard.

TSTA is available for guitar as a book w/CD, DVD, or DVD/book/CD Combo. For Bass Guitar as a Book w/CD and DVD. Spanish translation available for guitar.

978-0976291732

978-0976291749

COMPLETE GUITAR BY EAR
COMPLETE BASS GUITAR BY EAR
2 CD Relative Pitch Ear Training Courses

LEARN EVERY NOTE ON YOUR GUITAR or BASS COMPLETELY BY EAR! No written text or sheet music. Over 50 recorded lessons. A proven system that will help you develop a strong musical ear, finger strength and an understanding of music theory for guitar or bass. Just pop in the CDs and follow the lessons from your very first note to every note -on every fret -on every string.

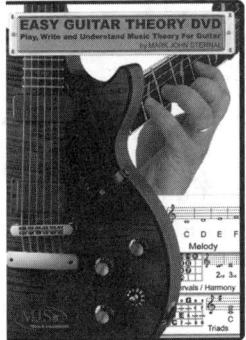
891926002090

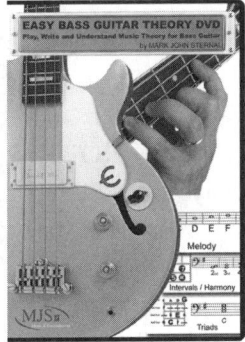
891926002083

EASY GUITAR THEORY DVD
EASY BASS GUITAR THEORY DVD
Play, Write and Understand Music Theory

After decades of dedicated music study and 17 years of teaching music, expert musician and educator Mark John Sternal has created a theory method that simplifies the foundations and structure for playing and writing music. Available for guitar or bass, EASY THEORY DVD contains all you need to know about music theory. Lesson material is presented in a progressive, easy to follow format that will be cherished by everyone from complete beginners to dedicated professionals.

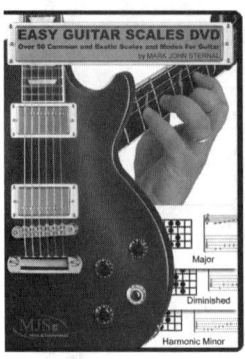
891926002021

891926002076

EASY GUITAR SCALES DVD
EASY BASS GUITAR SCALES DVD
Over 50 Common & Exotic Scales & Modes

Scales are the foundation of music and can be found in every known culture. With all styles of music, scales are the heartbeat, breath and soul of the solo, the riff and even the vocal melody. EASY SCALES, (for guitar or bass), includes every scale you've ever wanted to learn-presented in a simple root-to-octave format, starting with basic scales, such as major, minor, pentatonic and blues, and then progressing into patterns that span all musical styles and cultures.

891926002199

EASY ACOUSTIC GUITAR DVD: Beginner Basics and Beyond

FAST - FUN - EASY
This video features all acoustic instruments and gives the beginner guitarist all they need to survive in the world of acoustic guitar! The proven content was **designed by Expert Guitar Instructor Mark John Sternal** to be the **FASTEST** and **EASIEST** way to learn to play, **GUARANTEED!** The student will learn to read guitar music with notation, TAB and charts. The method is geared to allow the viewer to start playing instantly, learning **individual notes**, then progressively builds up from partial **two string** chords to full, **six string** chords. In part 3 of this video, the student will graduate to learn their first **5 SONGS** in the most popular music styles, including **Rock, Blues and Country!**

891926002144

EASY BLUES GUITAR DVD: Blues Guitar Lessons For Beginner Through Intermediate

If you want to learn to play Blues Guitar, look no further –You have found the ultimate course! Expert guitar instructor Mark John Sternal starts you out with simple power chords, riffs, tricks and techniques that form the backbone of Blues Guitar. Each lesson is introduced with thorough and descriptive instructions, followed by a slowed-down practice section which will insure that anyone, at any level, can play each exercise. These exercises are later combined to form complete Blues Songs. Each Blues Song and Blues Guitar Solo is presented at a slow, medium and fast tempo, allowing you to play along and build up your Blues Guitar Chops!

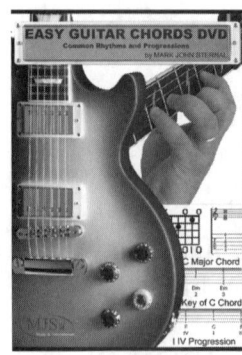
891926002038

EASY GUITAR CHORDS DVD: Common Rhythms and Progressions

Chords are the canvas for any song and any style of music. Using only 3 or 4 chords, guitarists can entertain an audience for hours! Whether a single player at a campfire, an afternoon on the front porch with friends and family, or an open blues jam, folk festival or stadium rock concert- all have one thing in common: CHORDS!
Easy Guitar Chords DVD teaches you easy, basic chords that are found in every key of music, starting with open chords and progressing with time, strength and practice to popular barre chords –all presented in a useful format that shows you how chords are used musically. By introducing rhythms and chord progressions, each section of this unique video course allows you to do more than learn just a handful of chords...you will actually learn to play and make music with them!

891926002106

EASY METAL GUITAR DVD: Heavy Metal Guitar Lessons For Beginner To Intermediate

If you want to learn to play Heavy Metal Guitar, look no further –You have found the ultimate course with EASY METAL GUITAR DVD! Start out with simple power chords, riffs, tricks and techniques that form the backbone of Heavy Metal Guitar Playing. Each lesson is introduced with thorough and descriptive instructions, followed by a slowed-down practice section which will insure that anyone, at any level, can play each exercise. These exercises are later combined to form complete Metal Songs. Each Metal Song and Metal Solo is presented at a slow, medium and fast tempo, allowing you to play along and build up your Metal Guitar Chops!

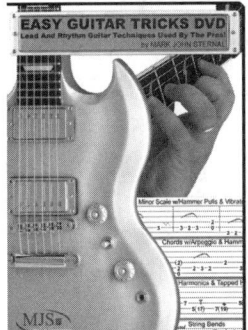

891926002151

EASY GUITAR TRICKS DVD: Lead And Rhythm Guitar Techniques Used By The Pros!

Learn to use the highly-guarded techniques of the guitar pros! Make each and every note count! Playing a note—or even a handful of notes—is one thing, but learning to give each note life, while making them sound tight, professional and desirable, is an important task to master. Using simple techniques that have taught thousands of eager students over the past 18 years, expert guitar instructor Mark John Sternal teaches you fun, useful guitar tricks quickly and easily. You'll be amazed at how, after learning a few basic guitar tricks and techniques, you'll never be at a loss when it comes to guitar playing—whether writing your own songs, playing cover tunes or improvising.

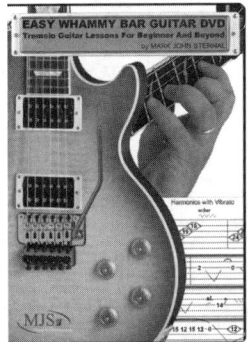

891926002182

EASY WHAMMY BAR GUITAR DVD: Tremolo Guitar Lessons For Beginner and Beyond

Some of the coolest sound effects in guitar history come from use of the whammy bar! Many guitars come equipped, but guitar players often avoid using them, or are very limited with what they can do with them. In EASY WHAMMY BAR GUITAR DVD, expert guitar instructor Mark John Sternal sends the viewer off on a 1-hour-39-minute exploration of this amazing guitar accessory.

Book/CD
978-0976291763

GUITAR: Probable Chords - a "Chord Key Encyclopedia"

Author Mark John Sternal has been credited as one of the greatest guitar teachers of the 21st Century! In his latest volume he sets out to achieve what no other music instruction publisher has ever accomplished. The expert reviews, along with thousands of raving customer testimonies are indication that he has surpassed his goal with GUITAR: Probable Chords.

The unique name comes from the investigative term Probable Cause, and like a crime scene investigator, Mark digs deep into the world of guitar chords. In this one of a kind chord method, he teaches you to use every chord, from basic structures to intermediate and advanced extensions and variations -in every key of music, and how to use them to write and play songs.

To learn more about these and other titles by Mark John Sternal, please visit **www.mjspublications.com**.

Blank Note Charts